OLIVE OATMAN

A COMPLETE LIFE FROM BEGINNING TO THE END

HISTORY HUB

Olive Oatman

A Complete Life from Beginning to the End

An Unauthorized Biography

History Hub

TABLE OF CONTENTS

Don't Forget Your Free Bonus Downloads!

As our way of saying thank you, we've included in **_every purchase_** bonus gift downloads. If you've enjoyed reading this book, please consider leaving a review.

Or Scan Your Phone to open QR code

CHAPTER ONE

Birth & Early Childhood

On September 7, 1837, Olive Ann Oatman was born in La Harpe, Illinois. She is one of seven children of Royce and Mary Ann Oatman, who were members of the Mormon church. Her father, Royce, started out as a farmer, and eventually became a business-owner. Unfortunately, there is little to no recorded information about Olive Oatman's childhood.

During the time Oatman was born, local landowners started building their town which they called "Franklin." As the town grew, they applied for a mail station, but the council informed them that another city in Illinois was already named Franklin. The postmaster, Louis Rice Chaffin, proposed "La Harpe" for their new town name, in honor of the French explorers who arrived and spent the winter there in 1715. The Illinois council granted the City of La Harpe a contract in 1859.

Another significant event that occurred during the time of Oatman's birth was The Panic of 1837. Inflation went out of control after federal deposits to the Second Bank of the United States were pulled back. There was suspicion that the administration was selling land for state monetary orders at questionable amounts. On May 10, 1837, each bank in New York City started to acknowledge installment in "hard cash," generally as gold and silver coinage, constraining a sensational, deflationary backfire. The Panic led to a five-year financial crisis laden with bank failures and high unemployment rates.

Conditions in the South were a lot worse than the states in the Northeast. In Virginia, North Carolina, and South Carolina, the Panic prompted expanded enthusiasm for broadening crops. New Orleans encountered a sharp decline in business and the state of its financial market remained negative all through 1843. Numerous planters in Mississippi had gone through a lot of their cash ahead of time, leading to a lot of business closures and bankruptcy. By 1839, a considerable lot of the estates couldn't proceed with development. Florida and Georgia did not feel the impact as early as Louisiana, Alabama, or Mississippi; be that as it may, they started to feel the Panic's harmful effects during the 1840s. The Western regions did not at first feel as much weight as the North or the South. Ohio, Indiana, and Illinois were agricultural states, and the plentiful harvests of 1837 helped keep industries afloat. By 1839, nonetheless, rural costs had fallen, and agriculturists felt the weight of the crisis.

This crisis led to Royce Oatman's decision to move in order to find a better life for his family.

CHAPTER TWO

Teenage and Adolescence

When she was 14 years old, the Oatman family joined a wagon train led by James Brewster, a member of The Church of Jesus Christ of Latter-day Saints (LDS Church). Brewster's followers were called "Brewsterites." They were bound for the Colorado River, now in Southern California, which was the "intended place of gathering" for the Mormons, according to Brewster. The Brewsterites had disagreements with the other Mormon group led by Brigham Young at Salt Lake City, Utah.

Around 90 people joined James Brewster and left Independence, Missouri, on August 5, 1850. Due to disagreements between the groups, they eventually split near Santa Fe, New Mexico. Royce Oatman and other families decided to head towards the southern route through Socorro and Tucson. In contrast, James Brewster and the remaining families travelled the opposite direction. Royce became in-charge of the group when they reached Socorro. Upon realizing that the climate in New Mexico would not fit their purpose, they abandoned their initial goal of going to the Colorado River.

When the group arrived in Maricopa Wells, located in Arizona, they realized that continuing the journey would be dangerous and unproductive. They would also be risking their lives if they encountered Native Americans living in the area who were not as welcoming towards the new settlers. Several families decided to stay except the Oatman family, who decided to continue their journey alone. Little did they know that this passage would be their last, as Native Americans would end up killing almost all of the family members near the banks of the Gila River, which is about eighty to ninety miles east of Yuma, present-day Arizona. This event became known as the Oatman Massacre.

People assumed that Olive and her sister Mary Ann were also killed by the Native Americans. The Yavapai tribe instead held the Oatman sibling's captive and turned them into slaves at a village near Congress, Arizona. A year later, they lived with the Mojave tribe after the Yavapai tribe traded-off the Oatman siblings for horses, blankets, and trinkets.

Together with the Mojave tribe, the Oatman siblings walked for several hundred miles and finally arrived at their new home, located at present-day Needles, California. Unlike the Yavapai tribe, the Mojave tribe treated the siblings as if they were part of the tribe. They welcomed them by tattooing their chins, a part of their tradition. Unfortunately, Mary Ann died due to starvation when an extreme drought occurred in Mojave village from 1855 to 1856.

Years later, rumors were circulating that a white girl was living with the Mojave tribe. A Yuma messenger arrived at the Mojave village, negotiating Olive's eventual release from the tribe and escorting her to Fort Yuma, located in Imperial County, California. When she arrived at Fort Yuma, she was welcomed back by her people and given new clothes by an officer's wife to replace the grass skirt she was still wearing at the time. Later on, she discovered that Lorenzo, her brother, survived the massacre and had been looking for her and Mary Ann. The reunion of the two siblings made the headlines across the West.

In 1857, Royal B. Stratton, a minister, composed a book about Olive and Mary Ann. It sold 30,000 copies and became one of the most successful books made during that period. In Stratton's text, Olive denied the rumor of being raped by the Yavapai. In the book, she said that "to the honor of these savages let it be said, they never offered the least unchaste abuse to me." Olive continued to live an ordinary life and got married to John B. Fairchild, a cattleman, in November 1865. They started the new chapter of their lives in Sherman, Texas, and adopted a baby girl named Mamie. That time in 1877, another rumor about Olive circulated again in 1877 that she died in an asylum in New York.

In 1981, Richard Dillon, a writer, announced in a well-known western magazine that Olive had told someone that she got married to the Mojave chief's child. According to him, Olive also gave birth to two young men when she got married to him. This record was not confirmed.

At the age of 65, Olive Oatman Fairchild died of cardiovascular failure on March 21, 1903. Her remains lie at the West Hill Cemetery in Sherman, Texas.

CHAPTER THREE

Career, professional, and family life

When Brewster's group disagreed with the others including the Oatman family, they decided to travel via the northern and southern route, respectively. In 1851, the group led by Royce Oatman reached Maricopa Wells, located in Arizona, where they learned that the trail ahead would be dangerous. Other families were afraid of passing there as the Native Americans currently inhabiting the land were hostile to the white settlers.

Only the Oatman family continued the trail because Royce Oatman was determined to find a better place for his wife and children. They did not know that on their fourth day, February 18, would be their last day together. A group of Yavapai tribesmen approached them and asked for food, guns, and tobacco, but their exchange turned sour. They attacked the family's caravan, killing Olive's parents Royce and Mary, along with her four siblings on the Gila Riverbanks, located at the east of Yuma, Arizona. Only

Olive and her siblings, Mary Ann and Lorenzo, survived in the massacre. Lorenzo had severe injuries that knocked him unconscious for an extended period. He was left for dead, but ultimately survived the ordeal.

When Lorenzo woke up from his injury, he found out that Olive and Mary were missing. Despite his injuries, he still managed to reach a place nearby to treat his wounds. After his recovery, Lorenzo continued to search for the bodies of his parents and siblings for three days. He assumed that her sisters, Olive and Mary Ann, were also killed in the attack. Little did he know that the tribesmen of Yavapai did not kill the siblings. Instead, they were abducted and forced into slave labor. The siblings worked to serve the tribe food, and carry water and firewood. Although they were beaten and mistreated, the siblings were kept alive to allow them to continue working for the tribe.

They served the Yavapai tribe for twelve months until the Mojave tribe visited the Yavapai village, and traded two horses, miscellaneous trinkets, and blankets for Olive and Mary Ann.

The Mojave village located near Needles; California became the new home of the Oatman sisters. Espianola, the leader of the tribe, adopted the Oatman sisters into his family and treated them well. They were even given their own plots of land to farm.

The Mojave tribe welcomed Olive and Mary Ann with a tattoo on their chins, as part of Mojave tradition. Their tattoo consists of five vertical lines in blue ink, with two triangles on both sides. According to the tribe, the symbol ensures that the bearer will have a good afterlife. Without it, the holder cannot go into the afterlife. Olive claimed that the Mojave tribe used tattoos to identify slaves in case they escaped the tribe, but the statement is far from the truth. The truth is, the symbols were only carried by people accepted and cared by the tribe for a peaceful afterlife. Unfortunately, the Mojave tribe experienced extreme drought from 1855 to 1856. Olive's sister, Mary Ann, was one of the casualties due to starvation.

Around 1855 to 1856, the United States Army received a tip that a white girl was living with the Mojave tribe. When she was 19 years old, a Yuma messenger went to the Mojave village and found her there. The messenger then reported on Olive's situation to Fort Yuma authorities. The post commander then requested for Olive's return. At first, the tribe denied the request and even told the messenger that Olive was not white. The tribe did this as they were affectionate towards Olive, and did not want her to leave. The messenger then sent horses and blankets in exchange for Olive, to no avail. Eventually, it ended in sending threats to the tribe, warning them that the army would destroy the tribe if they did not surrender Olive. And on February 28, 1856, Olive was released escorted by Topeka, the tribal leader, to Fort Yuma, where she met her brother, Lorenzo. Their reunion made headlines in the West.

Oatman moved to New York in 1858, and proceeded to live an ordinary life. She completed her education at the University of the Pacific, and married a cattleman named John Fairchild. They adopted a baby girl named Mamie, who grew up not learning about her mother's experience with the Native Americans.

Don't Forget Your Free Bonus Downloads!

As our way of saying thank you, we've included in **_every_ _purchase_** bonus gift downloads. If you've enjoyed reading this book, please consider leaving a review.

Or Scan Your Phone to open QR code

CHAPTER FOUR

The Person Behind the Fame

Main Difficulties to Overcome in Life

Olive Oatman spent almost all of her adolescent years facing difficulties and challenges. It all started when their family decided to relocate to another state. Royce Oatman wanted to find a better life for his family, leading to his decision to make the journey to New Mexico. They gathered in the spring of 1851 at Independence, Missouri, led by James Brewster. Royce did not know that his desire for a better life would be the reason for their tragic death. When the group of Brewster and Royce Oatman parted ways, Oatman changed their destination, and headed towards California. They traveled long distances under the sun's scorching heat and rough terrain. His oxen would collapse due to exhaustion, and even the other family members wanted to stop. Oatman was adamant to continue the journey because of his fear that his stock would perish before they reached California.

When they traversed the Gila River, eighty miles east of Yuma, around nineteen Yavapai tribesmen attacked them. It was a traumatic experience for Olive Oatman as she witnessed how the tribesmen smashed the heads of her parents and siblings with war clubs. Unfortunately, only Olive, Mary Ann, and Lorenzo would survive the ordeal.

The Oatman sisters were still grieving the loss of their family, but the hardships were only beginning. Even though the Yavapai tribesmen spared the sisters, they were abducted and turned into slaves of the Yavapai tribe. The situation became more difficult for them as they had to endure the mistreatment of the tribe and the death of their family at the same time. Facing slavery at an early age inflicted a deep-seated trauma in the sisters.

A year later, their suffering as slaves ended when the Mojave tribe arrived at the Yavapai village. The Yavapai traded the sisters off to the Mojave in exchange for goods, releasing them from their slavery. During their stay with the Mojave tribe, a severe drought struck the village in 1853, causing their crops to dry up, leading to famine. Olive's younger sister, Mary Ann, became one of the casualties of the drought. She died after she became too weak to accompany Olive in hunting seeds, roots, and grains. It became hard for Oatman because the last member of their family that she thought was still alive is now gone.

When she was 19, the Mojave tribe would eventually release her after a Yuma messenger went to their village and told the tribe that the post-commander requested Oatman to be in Fort Yuma. After a few days of her arrival, she was reunited with her brother, Lorenzo. Oatman revealed that she had nearly forgotten how to speak English after she stayed with the Mojave tribe for four years.

When she returned to Albany, New York, she attended school and quickly regained her mother tongue. Oatman and her story became the talk of the town. Richard Dillon, a magazine writer, said that Olive got married to the Mojave tribe chief's son and even gave birth to two young men. And when she moved to

Sherman, Texas with her husband, rumors circulated that she died

in an asylum in New York. All of which were untrue.

CHAPTER FIVE

Inspiration and Influence Behind Person and Work

Oatman faced many difficulties at an early age, yet she remained strong and overcame all these challenges. She could not have survived her later years without the inspiration or influence given by certain people.

Olive's parents showed strength and perseverance in the face of crisis. Her father, wanting a better life for his family, decided to make a long and arduous journey to California. During their trip, Oatman witnessed how her father, Royce, remained tough and carried on despite the numerous complications and hardships they faced. Olive, like her father, kept pushing through her very difficult adolescent years with the Yavapai tribe. She remained strong and survived despite the tragic death of her sister during the famine.

Oatman's release from the Mojave tribe led to a reunion with her brother, Lorenzo. For her, this could be the light from the tunnel that she waited for a long time. Their reunion reached headlines across the West because of Oatman's unique experience as a captive of Native American tribes. Royal Stratton, a Methodist reverend, had a significant influence on Oatman's life because of the book he wrote entitled "Life Among the Indians; Being an Interesting Narrative of the Captivity of the Oatman Girls." The book made Oatman famous across the country, and opened opportunities for her to reach her aspirations in life, such as finishing her education. Oatman received royalties from the book sales to complete her and Lorenzo's studies at the University of the Pacific. After they graduated, Olive Oatman and her brother, together with Stratton, moved to New York where they promoted the book. It became an opportunity for Oatman to tell her story and leave a mark on society. Lorenzo became her companion as they toured around the city. People became curious about Oatman and wanted to see the blue tattoo for themselves. Oatman became the first tattooed American woman ever known and was also one of the first female public speakers. During this period, the feminism movement was starting to develop. However, Oatman never claimed that she became part of the movement. Despite this, her story served as an inspiration for American women right after the Seneca Falls Convention.

Oatman met her husband, John Fairchild, during her lecture with Stratton in Michigan. Fairchild lost his brother after an attack by the Native Americans during a cattle drive in Arizona in 1854. That time, Oatman was living with the Mojave tribe. She got married to John Fairchild but never had children of their own. Instead, they adopted a baby girl named Mamie. Their family would move to Sherman, Texas. Olive would involve herself in a charity and a local orphanage where she was given the title "Sherman's Veiled Lady."

CHAPTER SIX

Main Accomplishment and Notable Achievements including societal impact and legacy

Olive Oatman became an instant celebrity when she arrived at Fort Yuma and her story made headlines across the West. Royal Stratton, a Methodist reverend, wrote an account of Olive and Mary Ann's story entitled "Life Among the Indians; Being an Interesting Narrative of the Captivity of the Oatman Girls." The book was published in 1857 and became very successful. Lorenzo and Olive received royalties from the book sales that allowed them to finish their education at the University of the Pacific. After their graduation, they moved to New York with Stratton to promote the book. Oatman toured around the city, sharing stories about her experience of being a captive as well as what she's learned about Native American traditions. Oatman denied all claims of sexual assault or involvement with any individuals from either tribe. Susan Thompson, a close friend whom Oatman later became reunited with—spread rumours that Olive had married a Mojave man and gave birth to two young men. Oatman embellished certain details in her lectures. She repeatedly told the crowd that the tribe inked her to recognize if she had escaped from captivity. She failed to state that most Mojave women also had facial tattoos, some with the exact same design as Oatman's. Oatman also identified her captors as Apaches, instead of Yavapai or Mojave. Nonetheless, Apache was a commonly used term to describe some of the Southwestern clans, so she may have been utilizing the word from that perspective. In these tours, she would remove the veil from her face to show-off the Mojave tribe tattoo. The tours ended when Oatman got married to Fairchild, who burned all their copies of Stratton's book.

Oatman quickly became a common household name within a month of her return, with updates on the salvage of the "young and beautiful American girl" showing up in papers across the country. With the success of Stratton's book, she became an even bigger celebrity. Journalists would usually write about Olive's appearance, bringing up her beauty as frequently as her tattoo.

Even though her name is not as well known today, Oatman's story or likeness is still referenced in pop culture today. There is a character loosely based on Olive named Eva Toole on the AMC show Hell on Wheels. Eva would have a similar backstory and would be sporting a similar chin tattoo. Oatman's story was also featured in a 1965 network show called Death Valley Days, featuring Shary Marshall as Olive Oatman—and including Ronald Reagan as an Army colonel who helped her brother find her. A book published in 2009 called The Blue Tattoo: The Life of Olive Oatman, recounted her experience. Olive Oatman is also the namesake of the city of Oatman, Arizona, near the Colorado River—close to the stie where Oatman was released after spending years with the Mojave tribe.

CHAPTER SEVEN

Interesting Facts

Did You Know?

Oatman's family was massacred at Gila Riverbanks near Yuma, Arizona. Oatman witnessed this tragic event during her adolescent years. This event was known as the Oatman Massacre. Olive together with her siblings, Mary Ann and Lorenzo, survived the massacre.

Did You Know?

The Oatman sisters became slaves of the Yavapai tribe. The Yavapai tribesmen beat and mistreated the sisters but kept them alive. A year after, the tribe traded the Oatman siblings to the Mojave tribe for their horses, vegetables, blankets, and trinkets.

Did You Know?

Olive Oatman became famous for her tattoo on her chin.
She acquired her tattoo as part of the Mojave tribe's
tradition, which symbolizes a peaceful afterlife.

Did You Know?

The Oatman sisters were treated well by the Mojave tribe. Espianola, the Mojave tribe chief, adopted the Oatman sisters and treated them as part of their family. They even gave the Oatman sisters their own plots of land to farm.

Did You Know?

Olive Oatman lost her sister, Mary Ann, to starvation. Mary Ann, unfortunately, starved to death due to a food shortage during the severe drought of 1855 to 1856.

Did You Know?

Oatman was eventually released and was returned to a regular life with her brother. When she was nineteen years old, she was released and escorted back to Fort Yuma, eventually reuniting with her long-lost brother, Lorenzo.

CHAPTER EIGHT

Discussion Questions

Olive Oatman was born from a family of Mormons. Describe the practices and beliefs of the Mormon religion. How did religion affect Oatman?

Discussion Questions

When Olive Oatman was born in La Harpe, the city was not yet fully established. Landowners of the city were starting to build the town, which they called "Franklin." How would you describe the town before it was developed? Was there a significant effect on the Oatman family?

Discussion Questions

During Oatman's early childhood, the whole country faced a financial crisis which affected most working Americans. Explain what happened during the Panic of 1837. How did it affect the Oatman family?

Discussion Questions

When the Panic of 1837 happened, Ohio, Indiana, and Illinois did not feel the impact as worse as the other states. What is the significance of being an agricultural state during this crisis? Why do you think other states experienced much worse?

Discussion Questions

The Oatman family lived in Illinois, which was less affected by the crisis because they are an agricultural state. Despite their advantage, do you think the family was greatly affected during the crisis? How did they handle the problem?

Discussion Questions

Olive Oatman's family had disagreements with other families and decided to part ways. Native Americans killed her family when they traveled via the southern route. What do you think will happen if the whole group decided to stick together despite their disagreements?

Discussion Questions

When the caravan encountered problems, Brewster decided to stick with the other group and traveled via the northern route. Why did Brewster side with another group instead of fixing the problem, given that he organized the trip? Do you think he still deserves to be a leader despite what he did?

Discussion Questions

The group led by Royce Oatman realized that continuing their journey could be dangerous and risky. Only the Oatman family decided to keep the trip, leaving the other families behind. Why do you think they decided to go even if it is dangerous and could risk their lives?

Discussion Questions

The Yavapai tribe traded the Oatman siblings for horses, blankets, and trinkets to the Mojave tribe. Olive became perfectly happy during her stay at the Mojave tribe. Years later, the tribe released her, and she returned to her people. What could be Olive's reaction and feelings regarding what happened to her?

Discussion Questions

Olive continued to live an ordinary life and then got married to a cattleman, John Fairchild. Several rumors about her were circulated, such as her death, and more. Why do you think Olive became the talk of the town several times?

Discussion Questions

When the group led by Royce Oatman reached Maricopa Wells, other families decided not to continue the trail due to the risk of encountering hostile Native Americans inhabiting the land. The Oatman family continued the trip because of Royce's determination. Why do you think the family continued instead of searching for other routes?

Discussion Questions

The Yavapai tribe traded the Oatman sisters to the Mojave tribe. Espianola adopted Olive and Mary Ann and even gave them plots of land. What do you think Espianola saw in on Olive and Mary Ann and treated them as part of the family?

Discussion Questions

Olive Oatman lived with the Mojave tribe until she was 19 years old. She was released after the Yuma messenger threatened the tribes with violence if they did not let go of Olive. Do you think there was a time that Olive wished for Whites to rescue her from the tribe? Why do you say so?

Discussion Questions

When the tribe released Oatman, she met her brother, Lorenzo, and moved to New York to live an ordinary life. She married John Fairfield and adopted a baby girl, who grew up without knowing her mother's past about the Mojave tribe. Why do you think Oatman chose not to disclose her past to her child?

Discussion Questions

Oatman spent the remaining years of her life in Albany, New York and in Sherman, Texas. Do you think there is a time that Oatman misses living with the Mojave tribe? If yes, what do you think she missed in the Mojave tribe?

Discussion Questions

The Yavapai tribe killed nearly all the Oatman family members, leaving Olive and Mary Ann alive. Instead, they captured them and held them as slaves. Do you think slave labor is the only reason why they kept the Oatman siblings alive? Explain your answer.

Discussion Questions

The Yavapai tribe kept Olive and Mary Ann in captivity for over a year. Do you think Olive and Mary Ann could have had a chance to escape? If yes, why did they decide to stay instead of fleeing from them?

Discussion Questions

When Oatman returned to live an ordinary life in New York and Texas, she became the talk of the town. How do you think Oatman handled the rumours circulating about her? If you were in Oatman's situation, how would you manage this situation?

Discussion Questions

At an early age, Oatman witnessed how the Yavapai tribe killed her family, experienced slavery, and saw her younger sister die due to starvation. What or who do you think pushed Oatman to become stronger to overcome this phase of her life? How do these challenges change her as a person?

Discussion Questions

The text described the life and tradition of both the Yavapai and Mojave tribes. It also mentioned the way they treated the Oatman sisters. Compare the two tribes.

Discussion Questions

Royce Oatman's strength and determination served as Olive's inspiration to stay strong in times of hardships. Do you have someone or something that influenced or inspired you when you were down? How did it affect you?

Discussion Questions

Oatman went to different cities and states to promote the book written by Stratton. People were curious about Oatman and wanted to see the blue tattoo on her chin for themselves. Do you think Oatman's story left a significant mark on these people, or was she just a morbid curiosity? Why do you say so?

Discussion Questions

When Oatman went around the city to give lectures on her story, the feminism movement started to develop. However, she mentioned that she never became part of the movement. Do you think there was a time Oatman became interested in joining the feminism movement? Explain your answer.

Discussion Questions

When Oatman moved with Fairchild to Sherman, Texas, she got involved in charity work and helped a local orphanage. Who or what do you think influenced Oatman to be part of these works? Why do you say so?

Discussion Questions

The text mentioned several people who inspired or influenced Oatman. Each person had their ways of showing their help and support. Who do you think had the most significant contribution or influence on Oatman's life?

Discussion Questions

Olive Oatman became an instant celebrity after her reunion with her long-lost brother, Lorenzo. Stratton even wrote a book about the Oatman sisters. Why do you think people got interested in Oatman so much?

Discussion Questions

The Mojave tribe adopted the Oatman sisters and treated her well. However, Oatman mentioned that the tribe inked her to recognize her if she escaped from the tribe. Despite the tribe's dignified treatment, why do you think Oatman released such a statement against them?

Discussion Questions

Susan Thompson, Oatman's best friend, spread rumours that Oatman had married a Mojave man and gave birth to two young men. Do you think Thompson betrayed Oatman?

Discussion Questions

Years after her release, Oatman married John Fairchild. Oatman's book tours came to an end after Fairchild burned all the copies of Stratton's book. Why do you think Fairchild did this?

Discussion Questions

At the peak of Oatman's popularity, journalists frequently wrote about her beauty and chin tattoo. What do you think Olive thought about this?

Don't Forget Your Free Bonus Downloads!

As our way of saying thank you, we've included in **_every purchase_** bonus gift downloads. If you've enjoyed reading this book, please consider leaving a review.

Or Scan Your Phone to open QR code

Dear reader,

It was my utmost privilege performing a deep dive to bringing this book for you today.

Before saying goodbye, I'd like to take opportunity to offer you one final gift. If you've enjoyed this book, may I ask for a small favor of a review?

Even a few sentences would help a lot and tell others more about this book.

If you do, as a way of showing my utmost appreciation,I'll send you for FREE a most cherished and valuable gift:

Top 7 Bestsellers Treasure Box

These are my personal bestsellers sold at bookstores valued at ~$30USD, my gift to you absolutely FREE.

To claim your gift:

1. Leave a review where the book was purchased
2. Send a screenshot to irvinepress@mail.com
3. Receive your gift of **Top 7 Bestsellers Treasure Box**

We've prepared the best and hope you'll find this offer exciting! Hope to see you again soon.

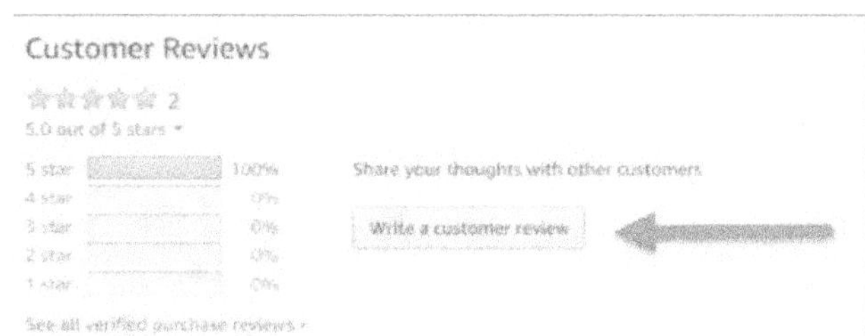

THANK YOU

Ways to Continue Your Reading

EVERY month, our team runs through a wide selection of books to pick the best titles for readers and reading groups, and promotes these titles to our thousands of readers – sometimes with free downloads, sale dates, and additional brochures.

Want to register yourself or a book group? It's free and takes 1-click.

Thank You

9 798224 341337